This book belongs to

_____

A B C D E F G
H I J K L M N O
P Q R S T U V
W X Y Z

This is a Dressy Countess Book
First Published in 2016

www.dressycountess.com

All rights reserved. No part of this publication maybe reproduced, stored in a retrieval system, or transmitted in any form or by any means, electronic, mechanical, photocopying, recording or otherwise, without the prior consent of the copyright owner(Dressy Countess).

ISBN 978-0-9948772-1-5

Printed in U.S.A.

That's All Me.

Written by Mia D.

Illustrated by Dressy Countess

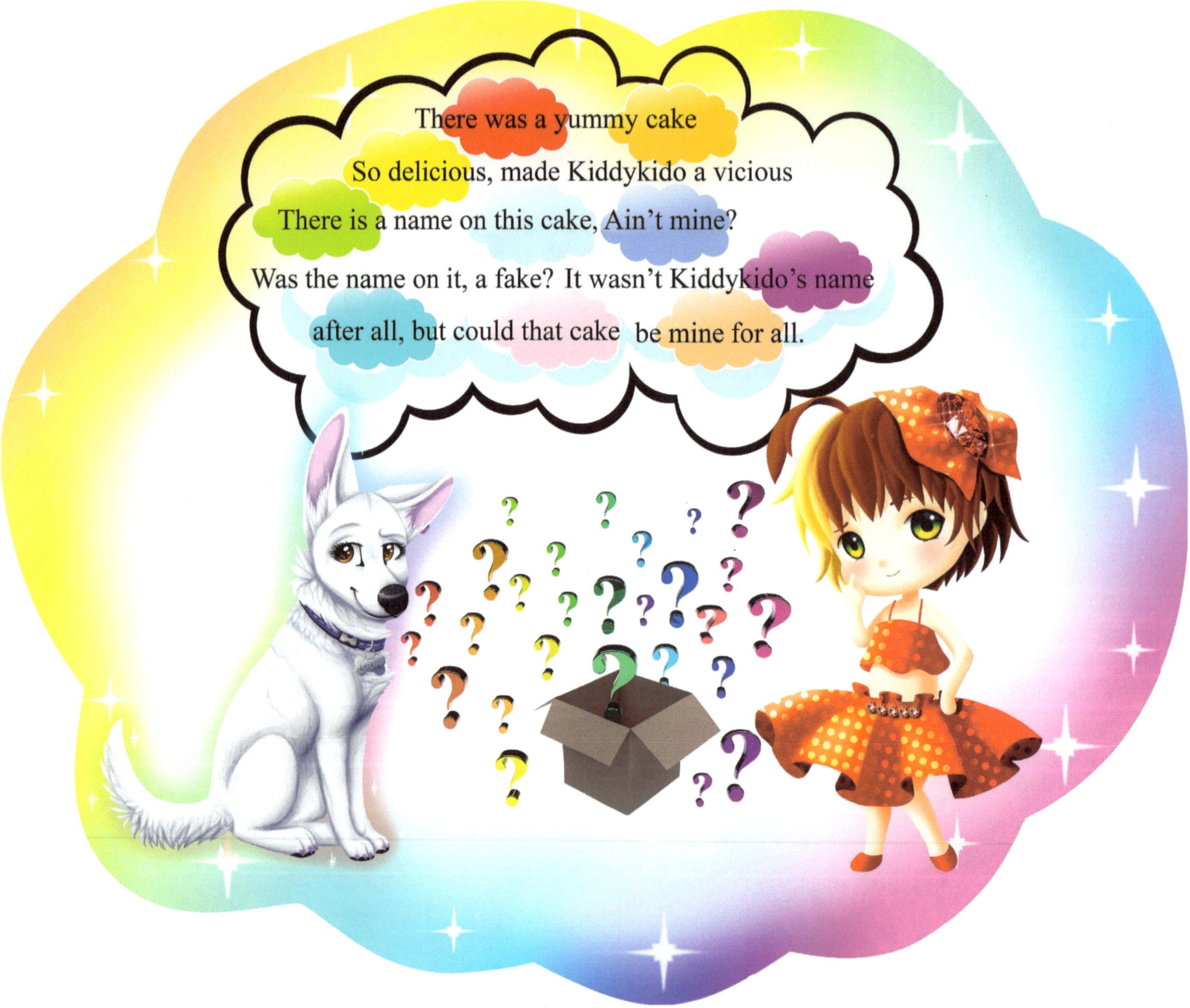
There was a yummy cake
So delicious, made Kiddykido a vicious
There is a name on this cake, Ain't mine?
Was the name on it, a fake? It wasn't Kiddykido's name
after all, but could that cake be mine for all.

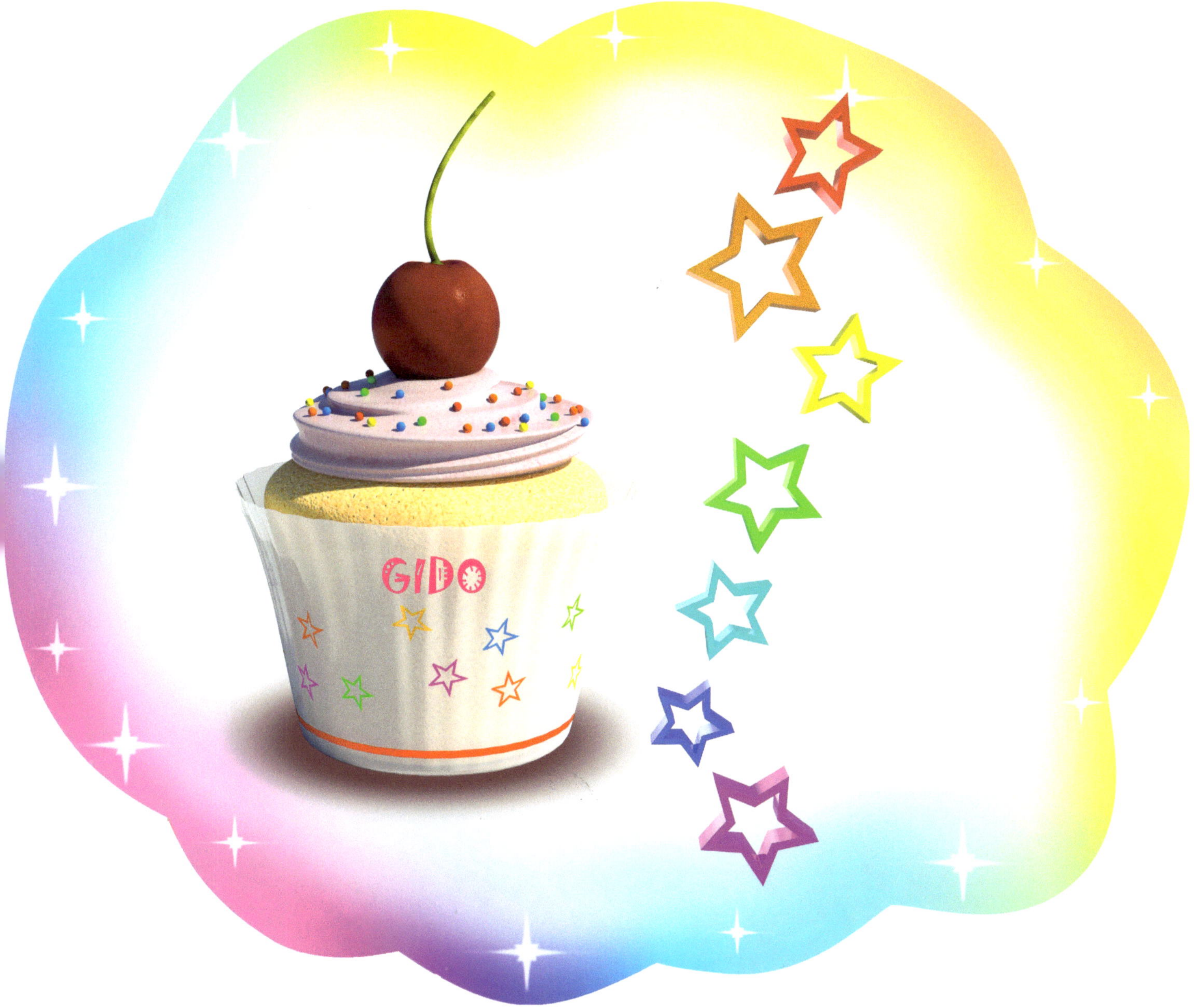
GIDO

Mom said:

"There is a Coontassi feeling in the air,
Something bad will happen, I am afraid..."
Coontassi told Kiddykido:"Put your hand on its edge,
have a taste, you look pale! Just steer, don't have
fear. You end up with no tear." Kiddykido said:"She is right,
though, not so bright. Sometimes says things that
isn't right." Had her finger on the cake. Tasted great!
Had no shame! Birthday cake did not look the same.
Mom was ready to blame.

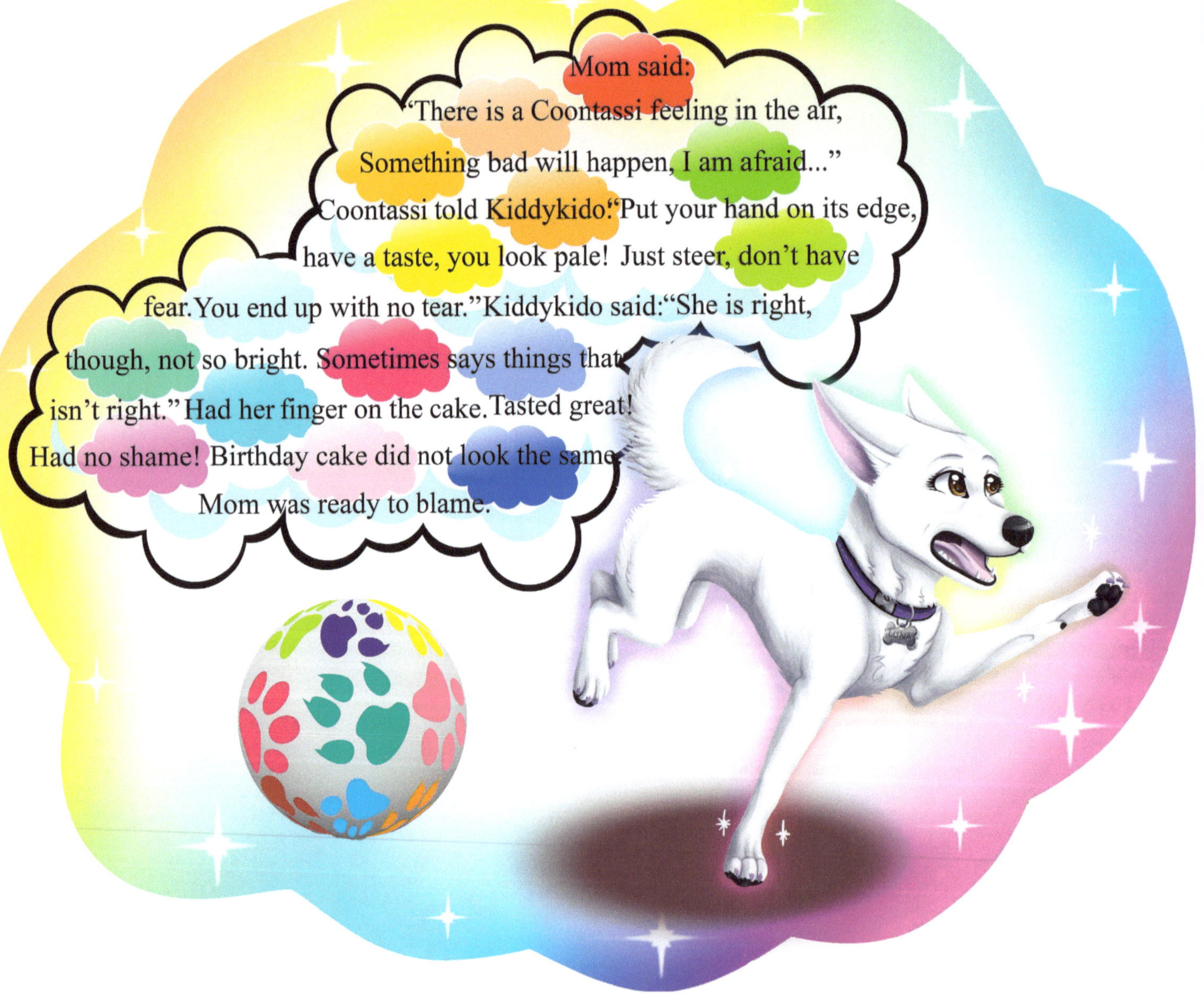

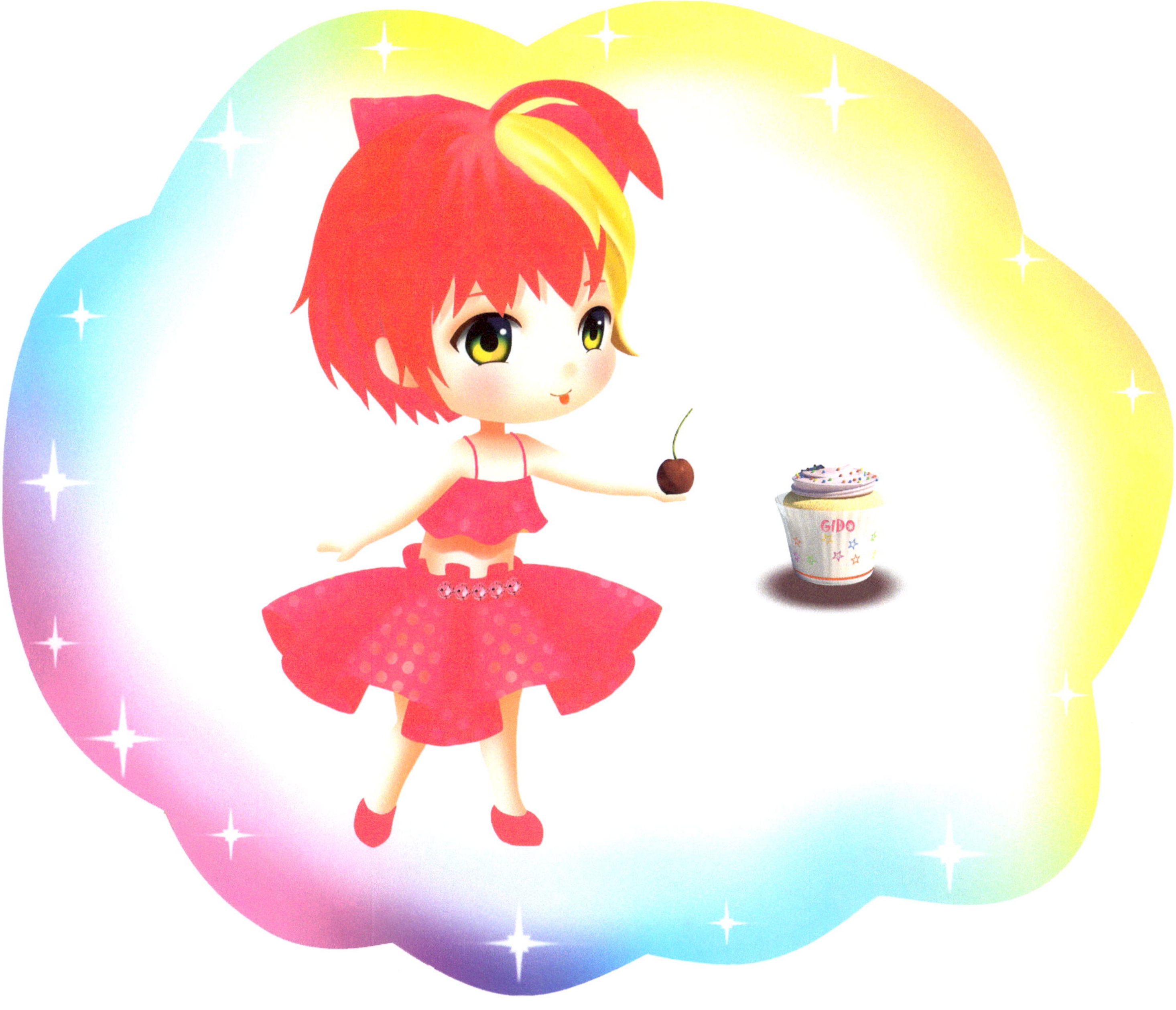
GIDO

Kiddykido was having lunch

Nice spaghetti with mini meatballs.

She looked at the back of her spoon to see what would

her other has to say. Coontassi came to view and said:

You look very attractive.

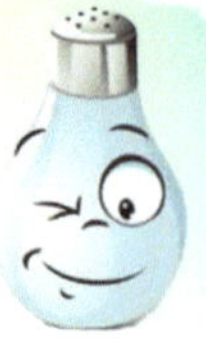

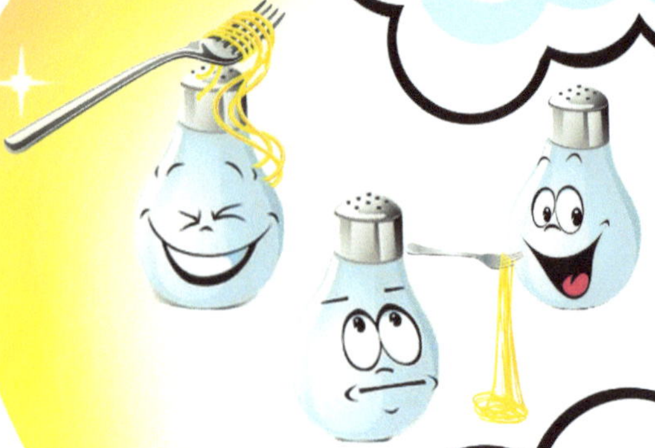

I just like to stare at you. You are so perfect.

But you wear lots of pink, something for you to think.

Maybe some orange and red, on your little pink dress

This sauce has a perfect blend.

It takes the edge off that pink!

Coontassi said: You are so good looking now

I can see a real art on your dress!

But maybe mom does not feel the same!

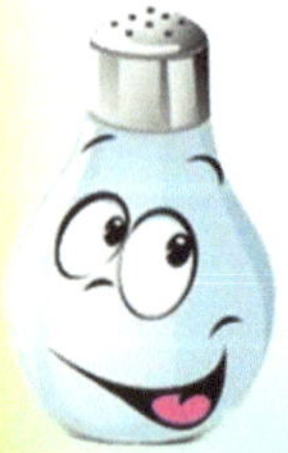

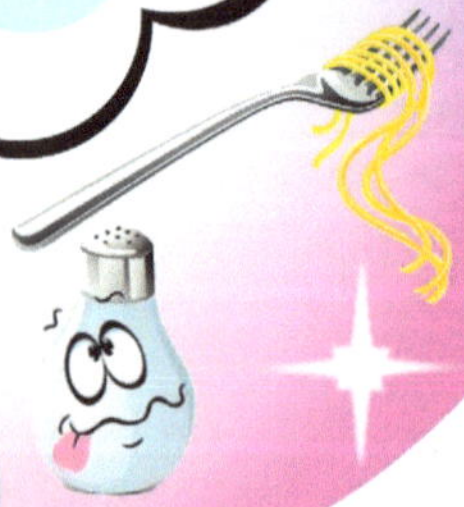

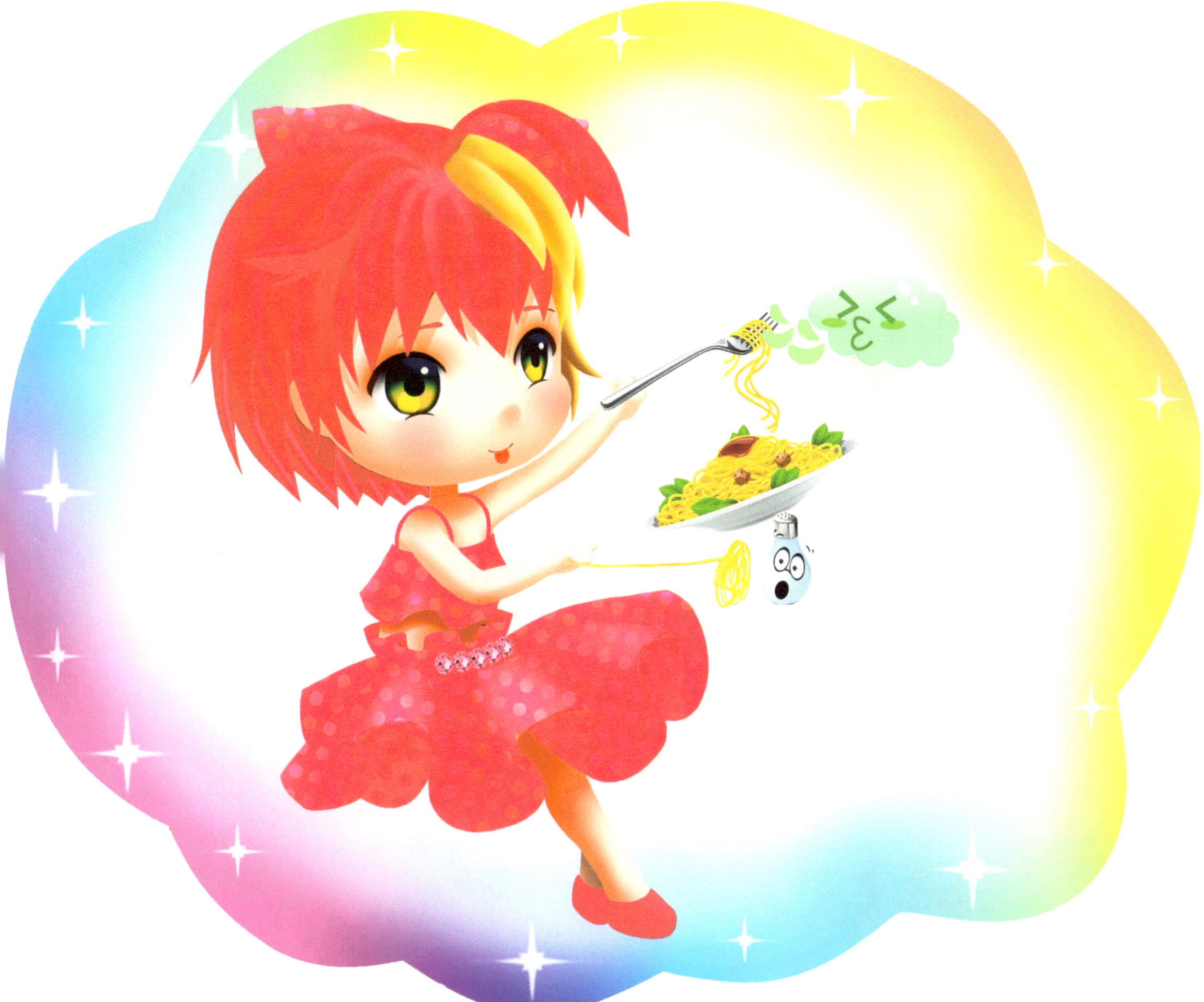

Mom said:
Watch the jelly bean jar, if you touch, it might fall
Mom left...With a drift. Coontassi came with flames.
Coontassi said: Um Um, no mom, tick tack.
Let's have, some fun!

Coontassi said:
Kiddykido let's have a share. It seems so fair.
Jelly bean jar was on floor, little beans were decor!
Mom said:"Can make this O.K. too!"
Please don't make it another two!"

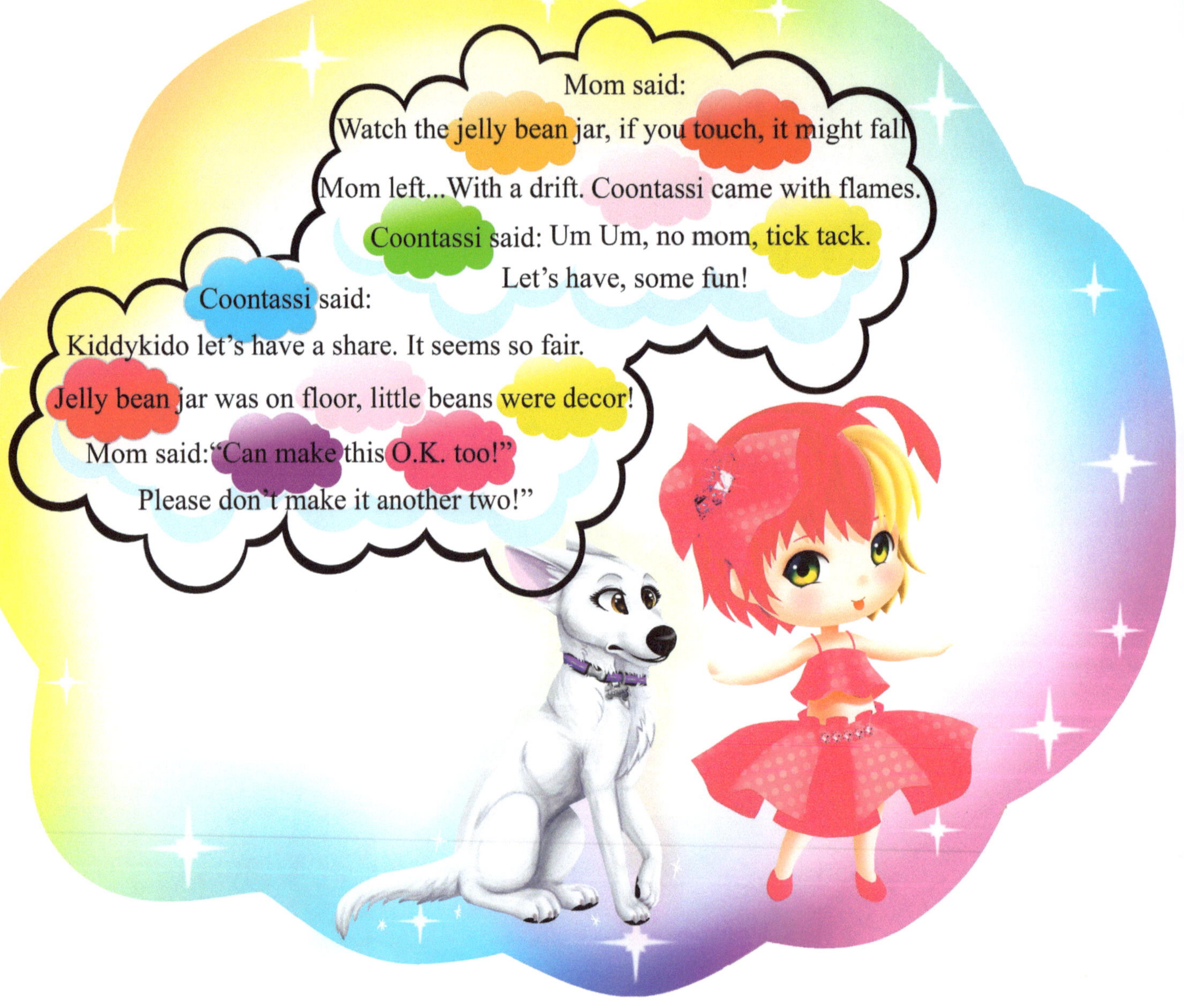

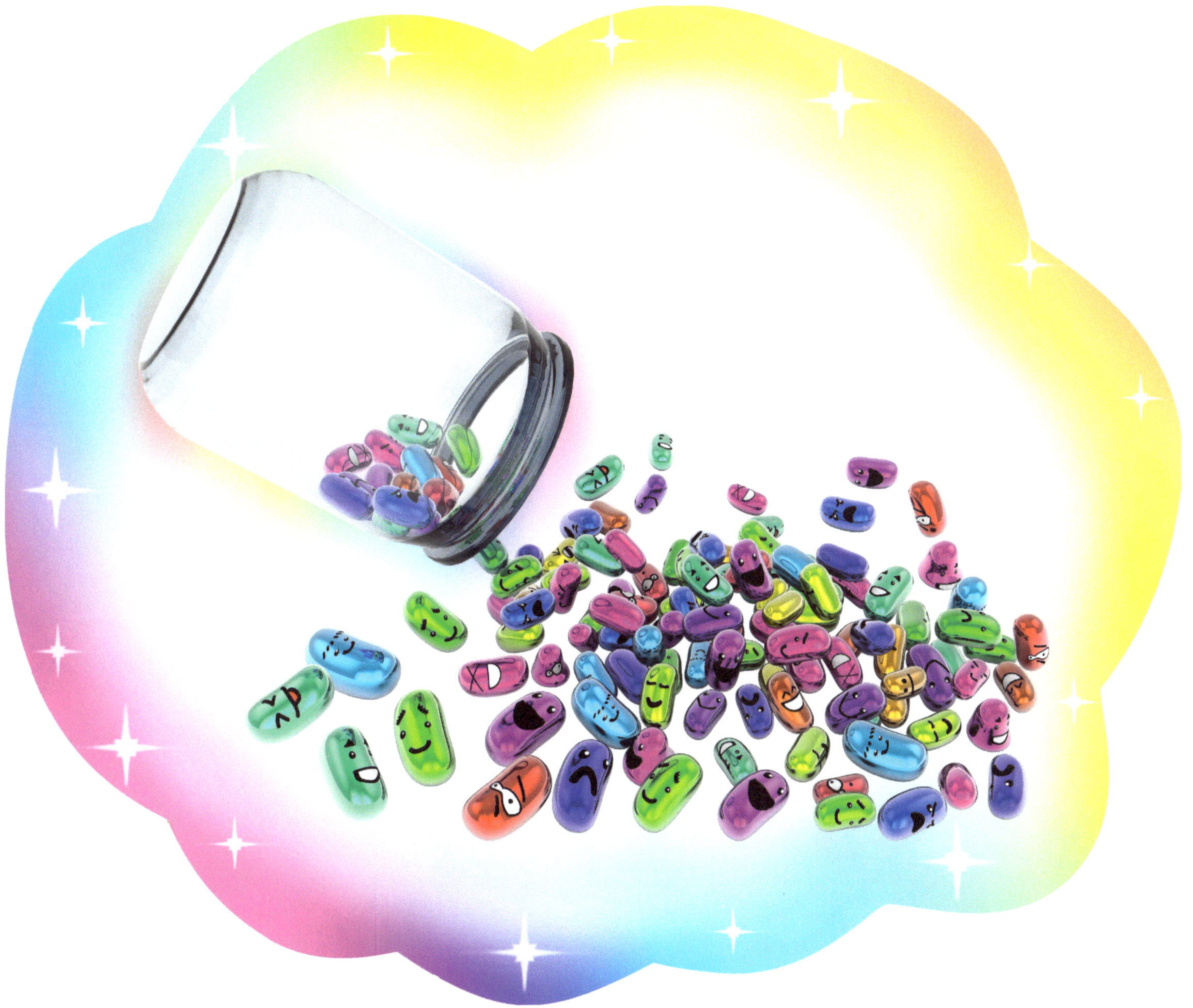

Kiddykido went to the shop
with her mom. Coontassi came along.
Coontassi said: “There , there... is that a pyramid?”
Kiddykido said: “That is a big orange pile!”
One orange was a bit too large.

Coontassi said:
“The low orange looked the best of all.
Let’s show that to mom. She will be flattered!”
So Kiddykido pull the orange off that point...But....
It didn’t make mom happy at all!

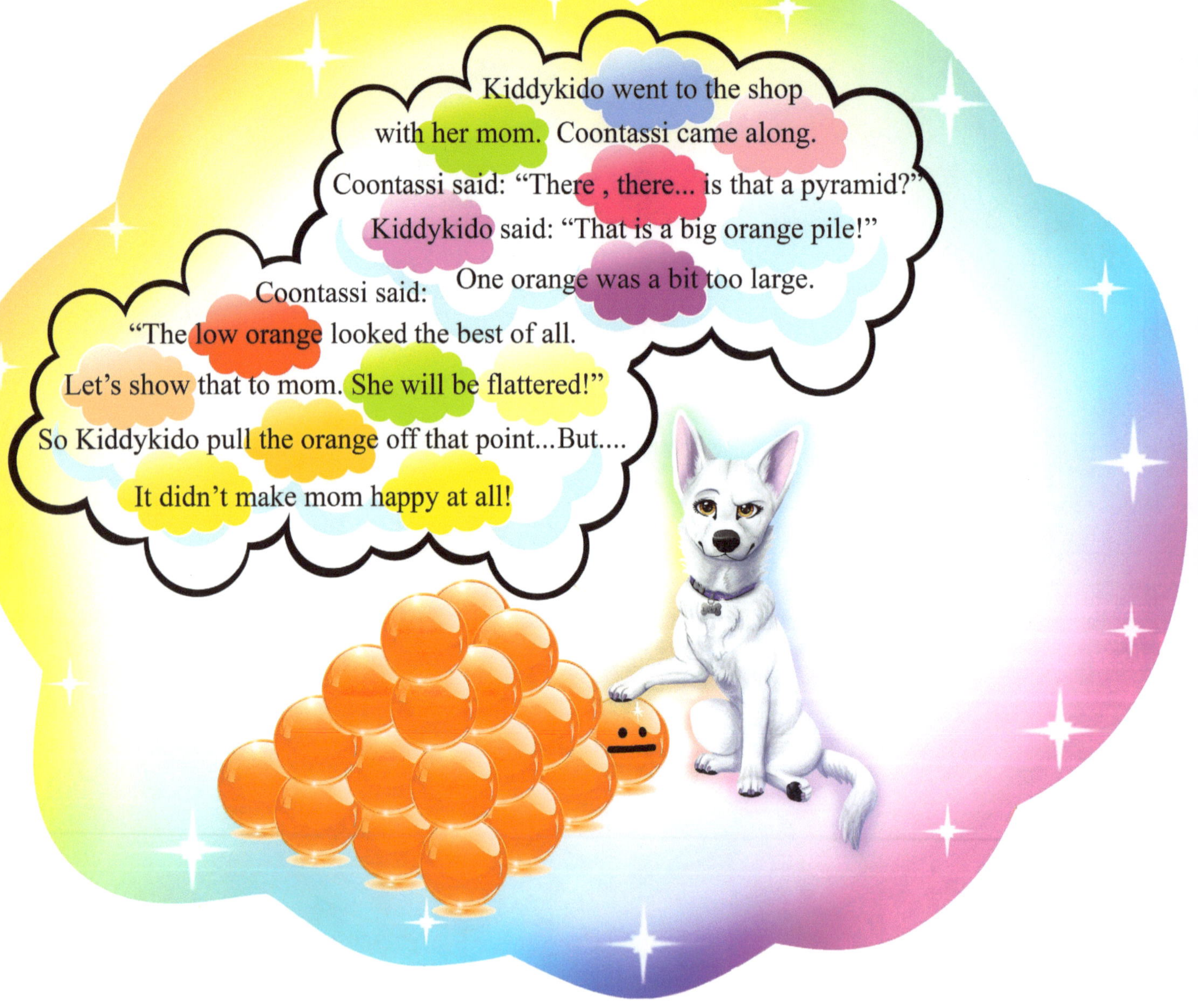

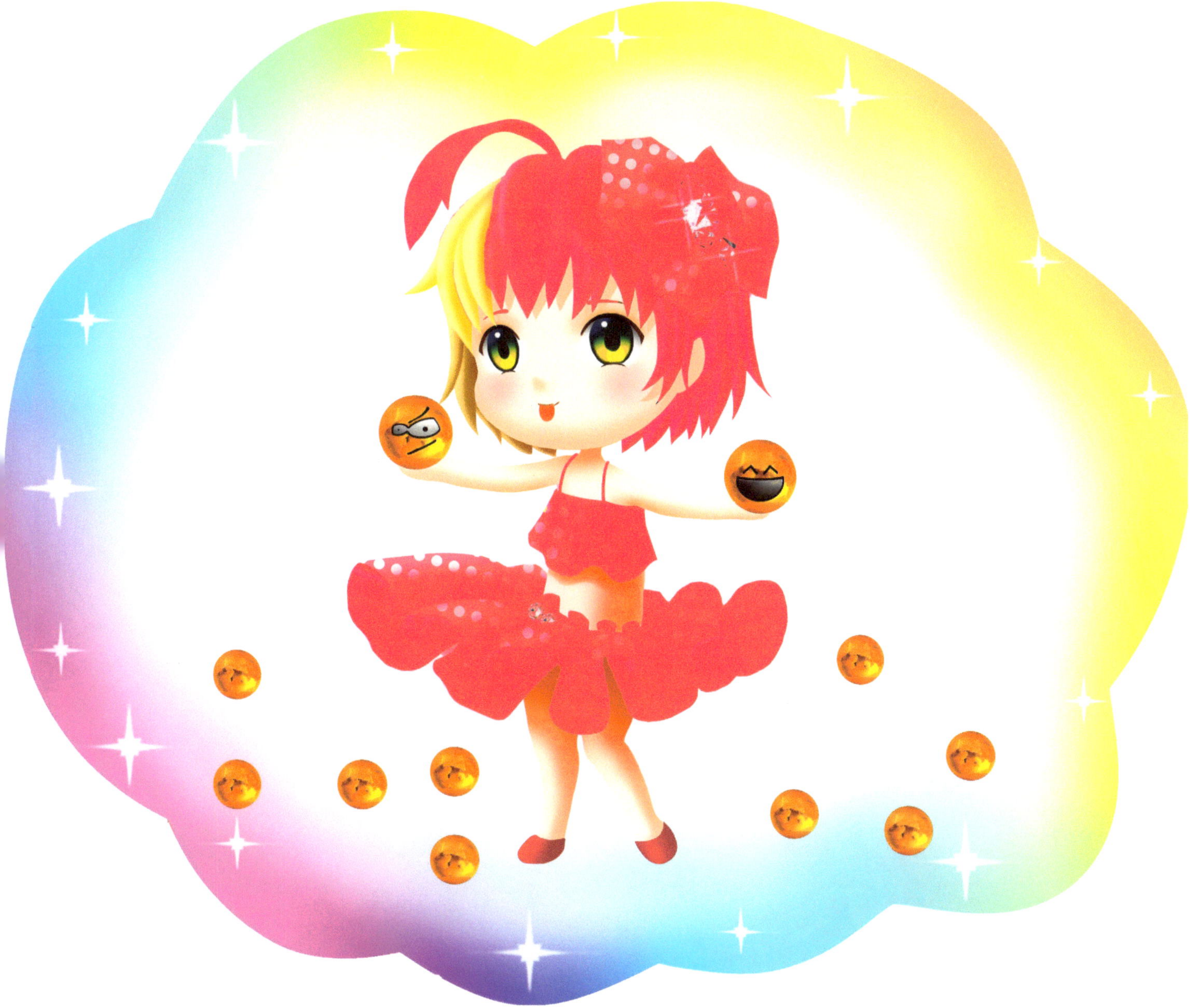

Kiddykido was having happy lollipops.
One for her, and maybe one for her little pal… Coontassi.
Having a lime flavor today and an orange tomorrow.
But Coontassi wanted a taste of all. Don't think twice. It's all right.
Would twice be too much??! Baby teeth weren't happy at all.

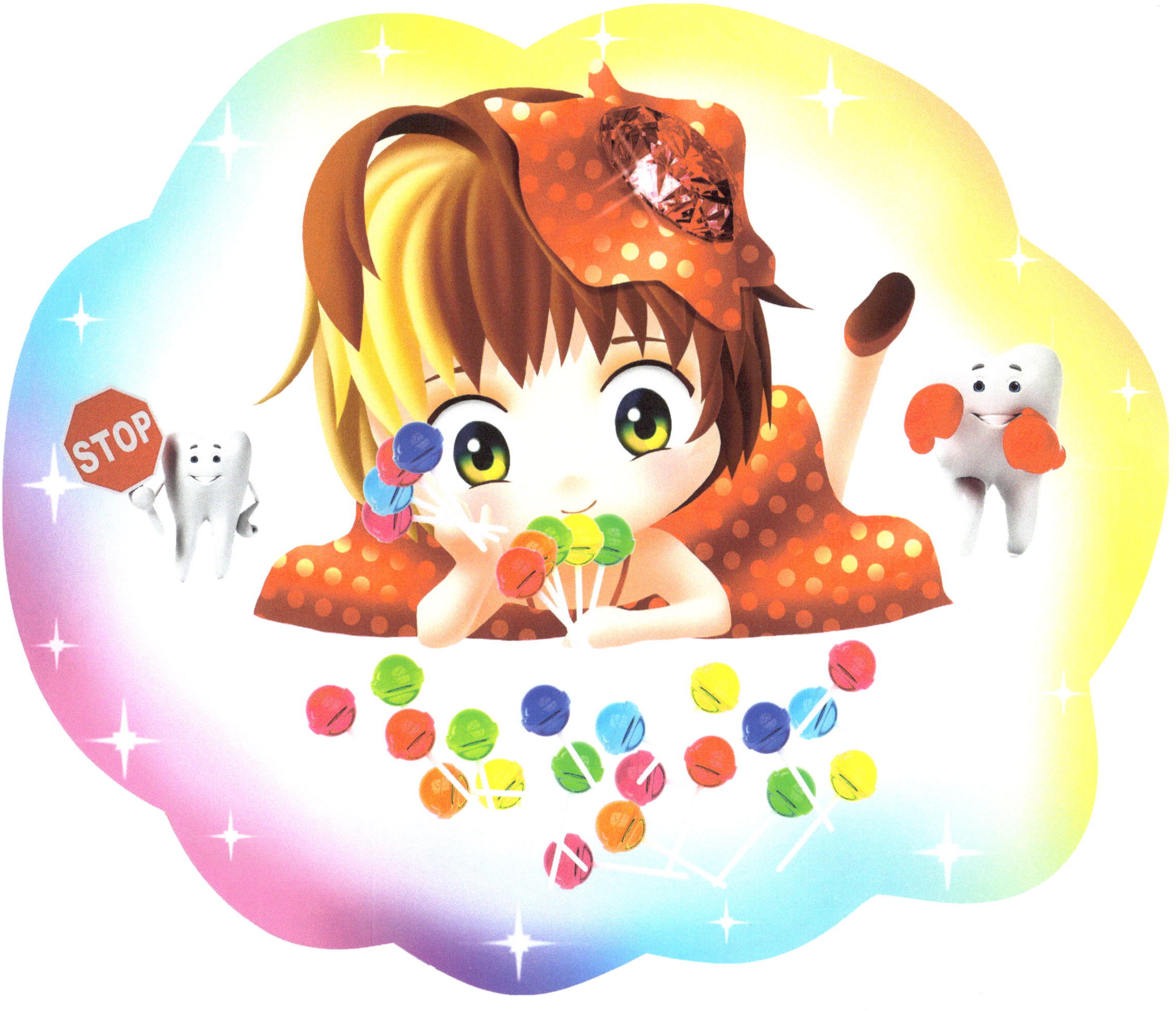
STOP

Kiddykido went to practice with her pals.

"What rules... I think I know them all!" She whispered.

Each time the coach called heads up. Coontassi kept her little head up. She got a bad hit by a free throw on her head.

Dizzy Kiddykido finally said: What did heads up mean again??!!

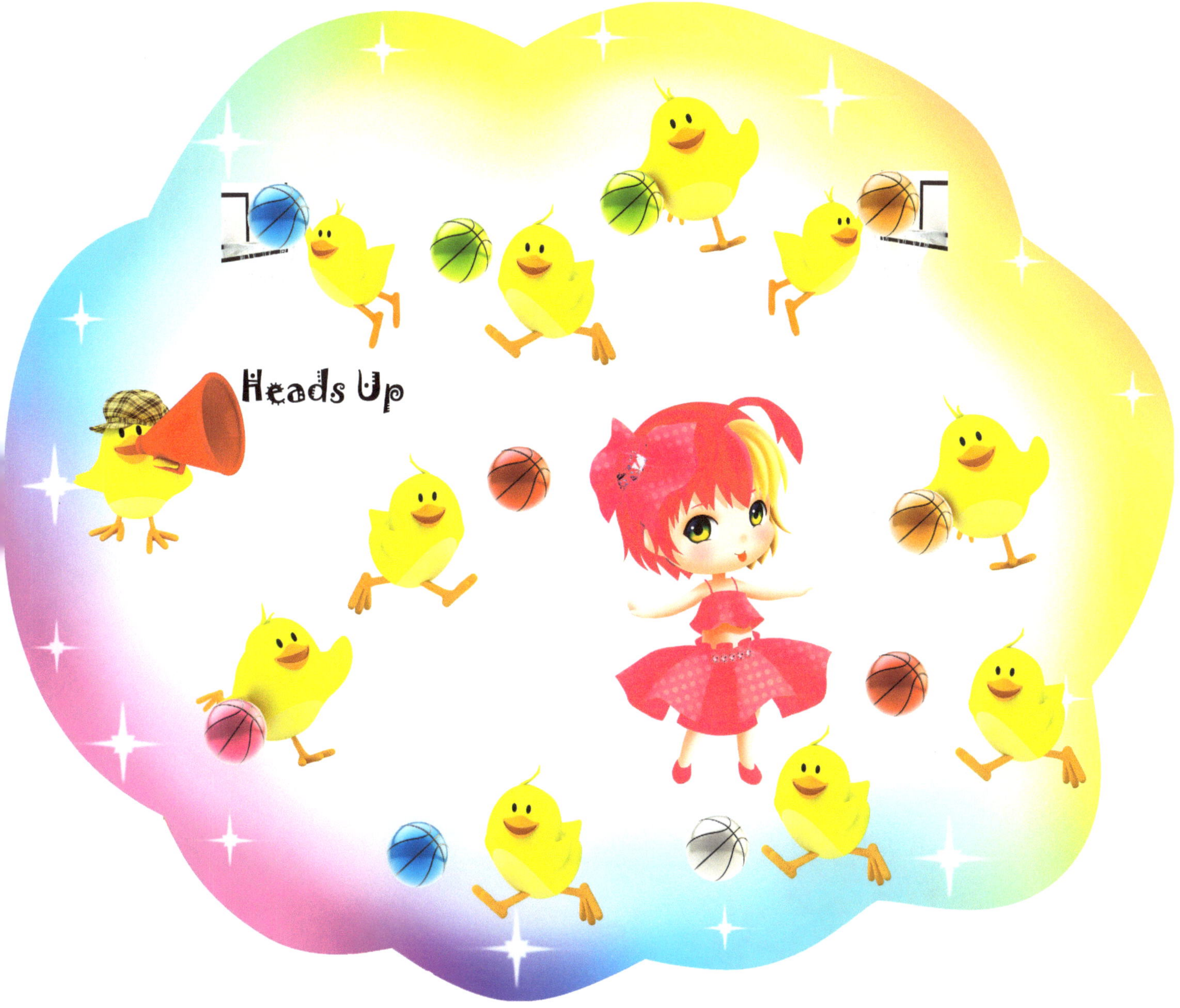
Heads Up

Bubbles are fun. I can make a ton.

My feelings are clear, I cannot be any happier.

Coontassi wants to invent: “Flying Chocolate Bubbles.”

“I can jump up, for some good grub.” Chocolate sauce fountain on display. Brown was the color of the day.

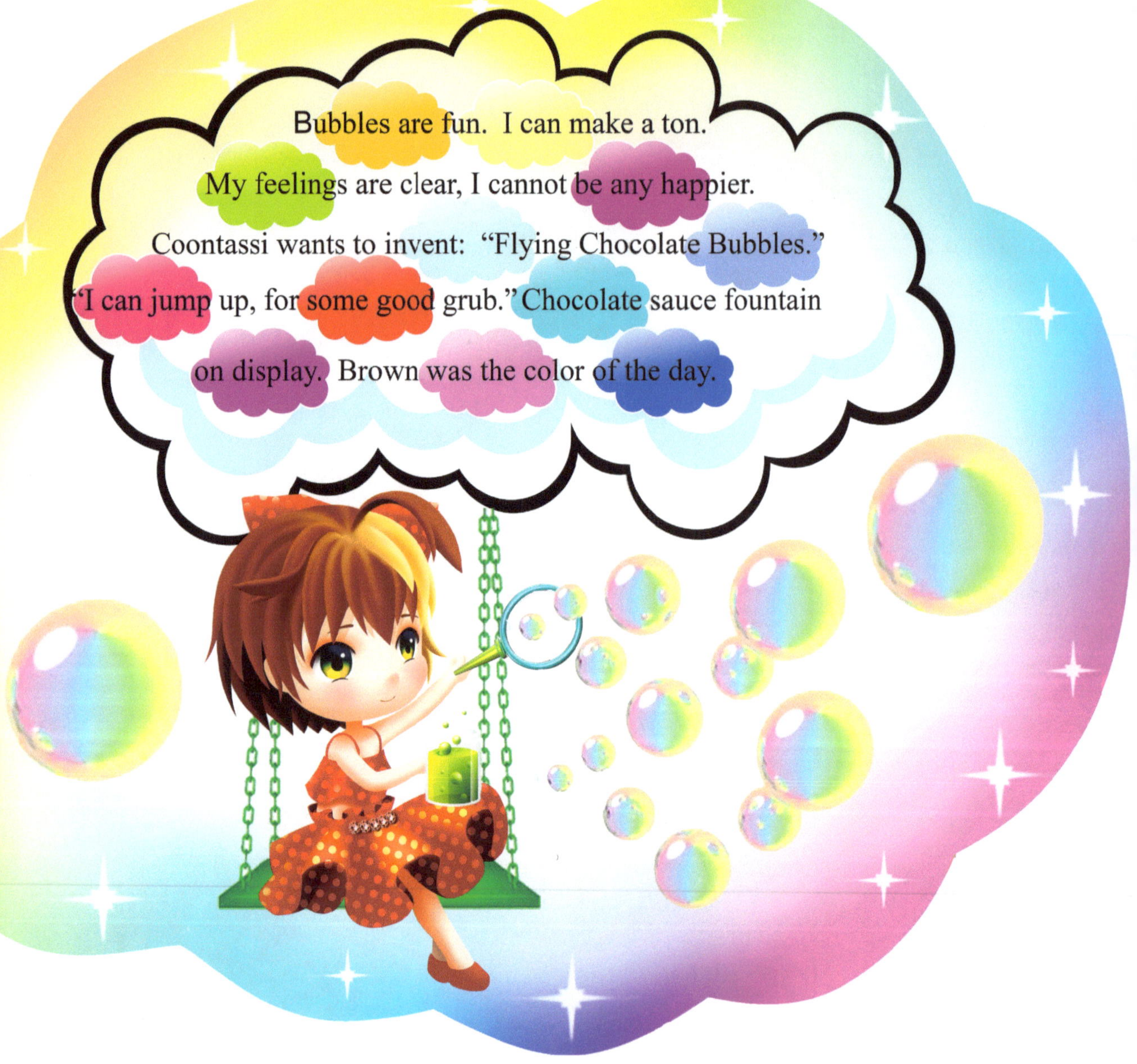

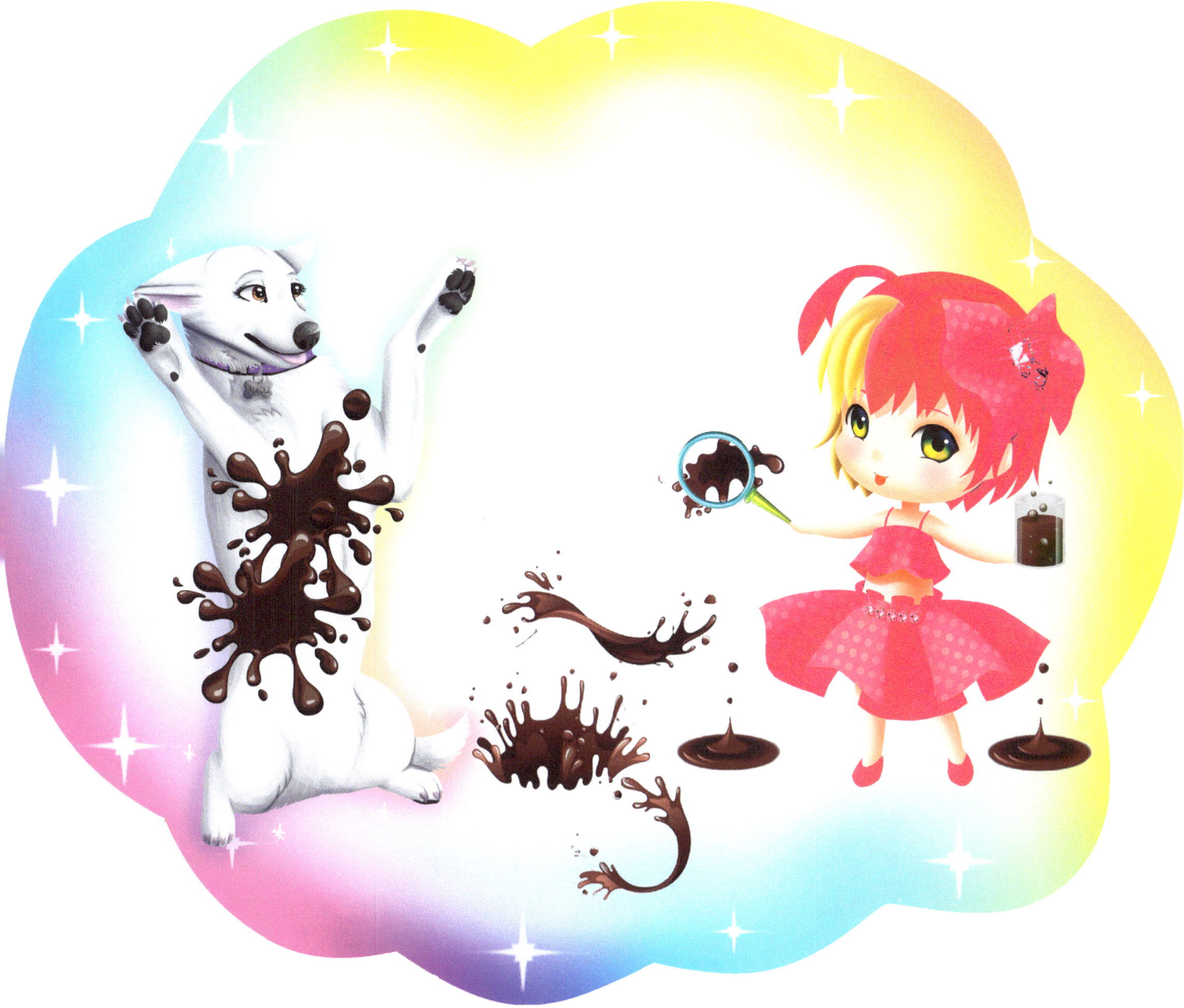

Kiddykido became upset
like a little mouse. Because of a
little Coontassi who was still in the house. Mom said:
“It is O.K. this time, please don’t listen to Coontassi on your
next.” Coontassi is back again, telling Kiddykido: “Remember
the Cheerios we shared, Fruit loops and the crispy little chips,
just give me another chance!”

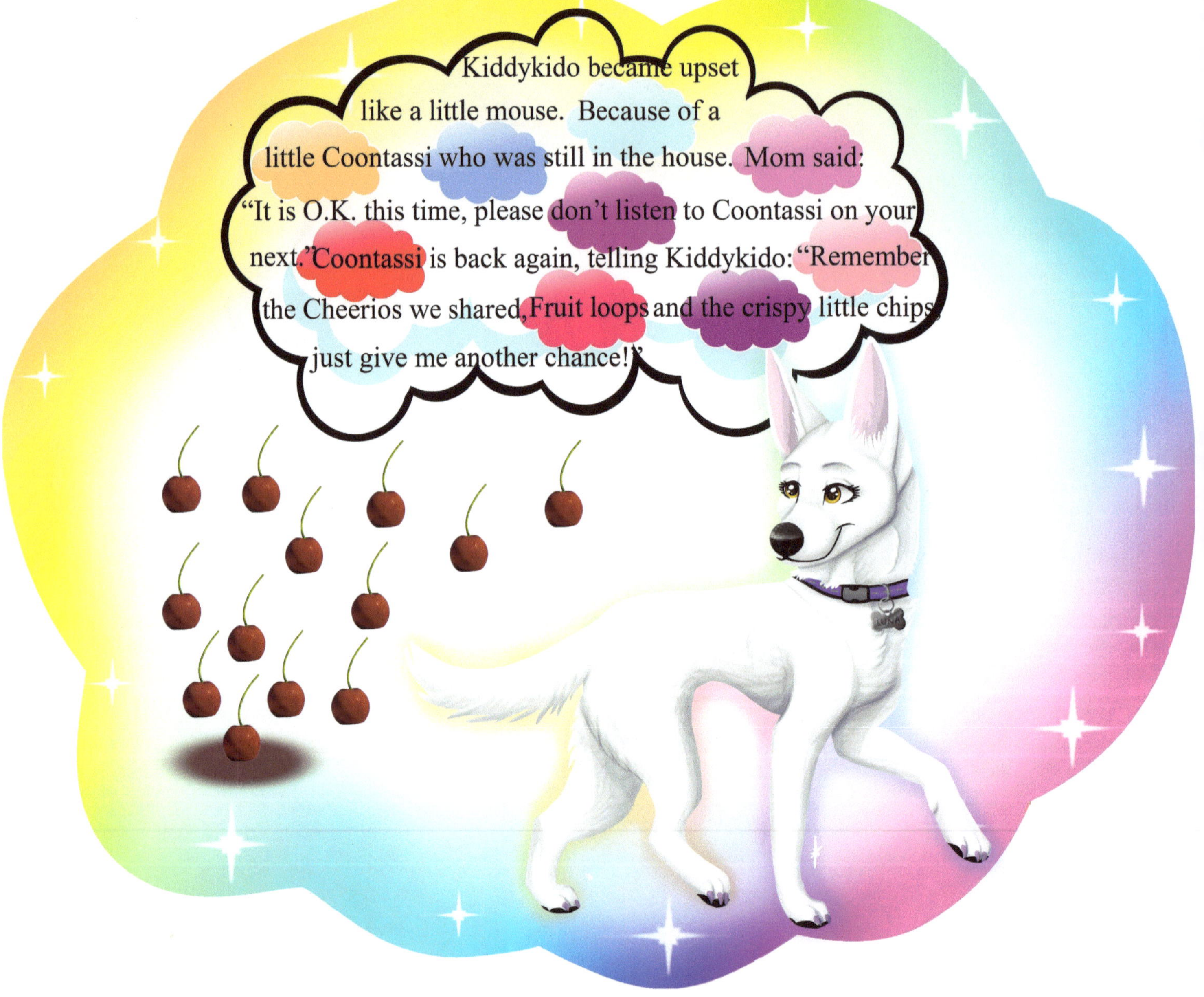

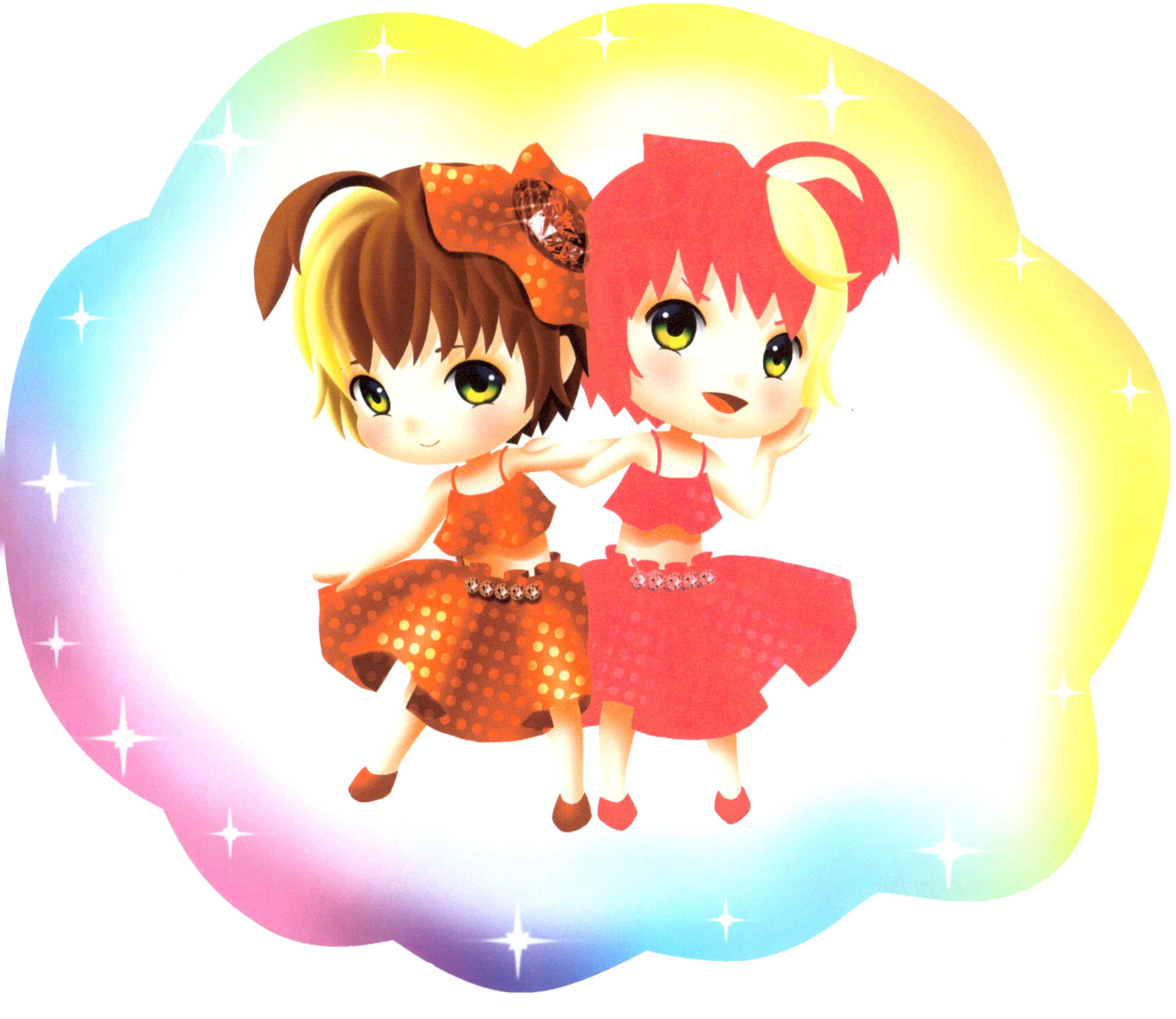

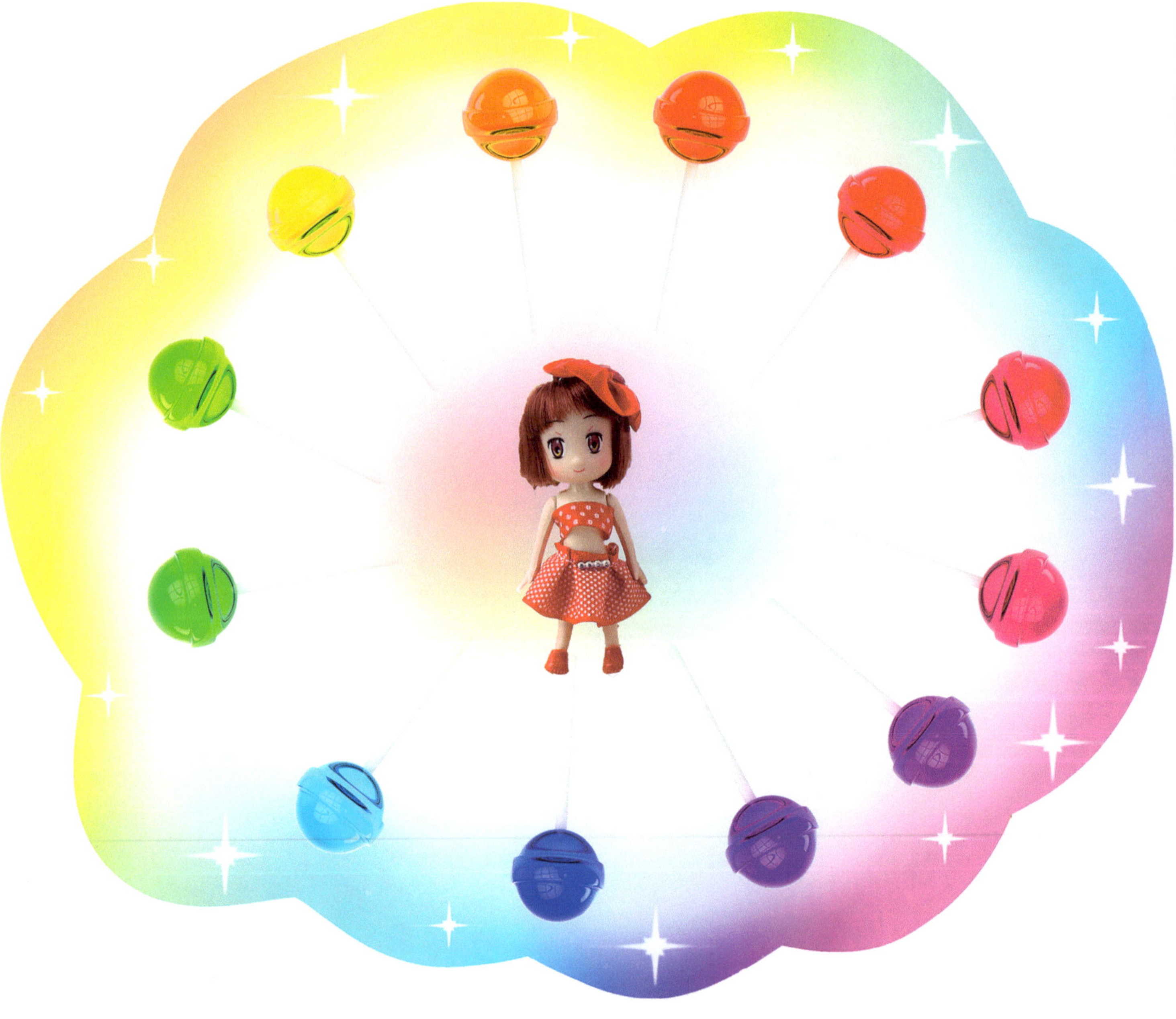

Things Coontassi told me to do, but I am not going to!

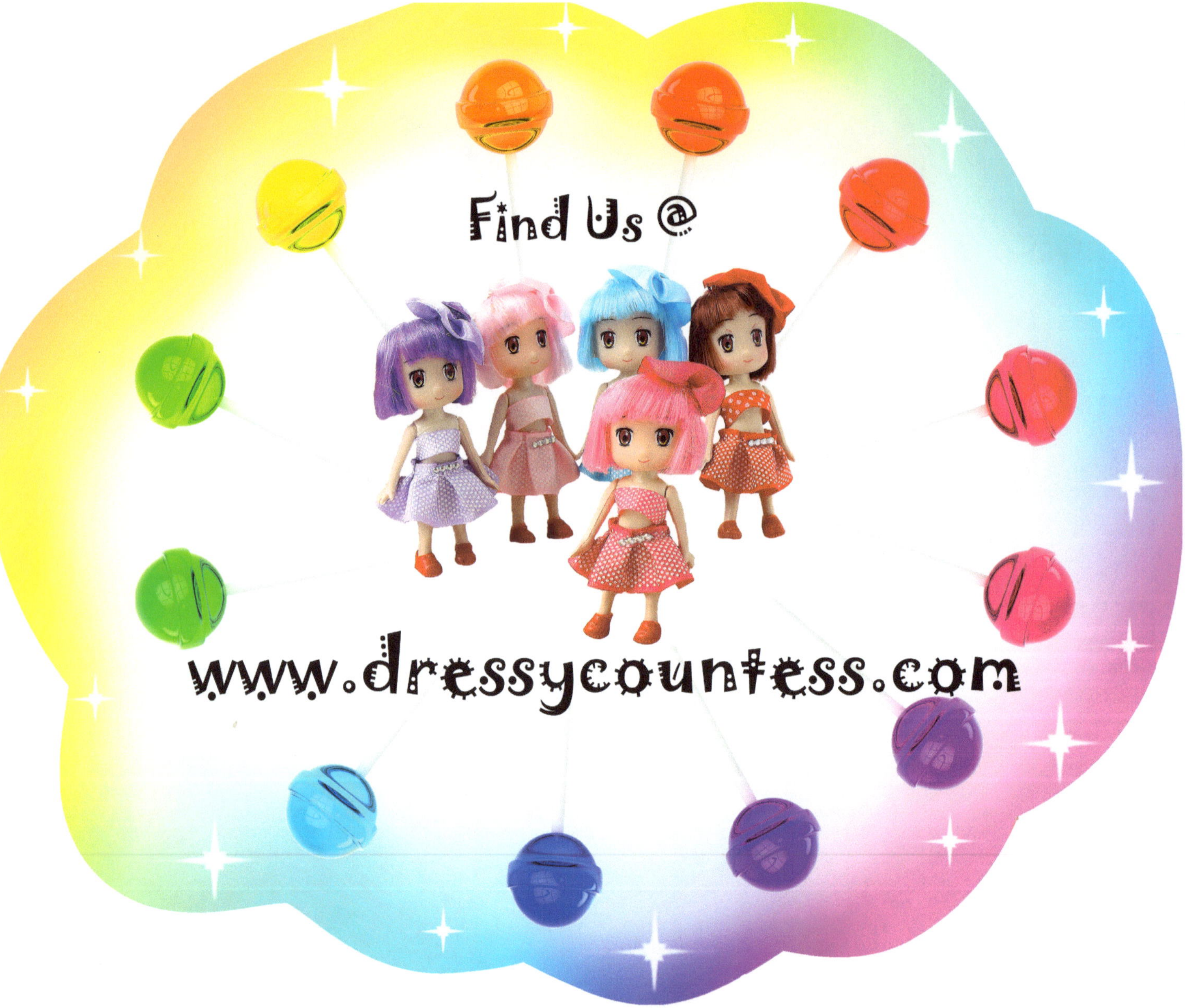
Find Us @
www.dressycountess.com

www.ingramcontent.com/pod-product-compliance
Lightning Source LLC
Chambersburg PA
CBHW041233040426
42444CB00002B/149